Calma Llama

Written & Illustrated By
Emily Hayes

Calma Llama

Written & Illustrated By
Emily Hayes

Over the ocean, way up high
Where snowy mountains touch the sky,
I live with my family in a herd.
I'm called Calma Llama, the third.

My woolly coat is wintery white.
It keeps me warm on cold nights.
But though I may look big and bold,
I lost my confidence, I've been told.

It truly was a mystery
And happened very suddenly.
The anxiety had just appeared
And filled my mind with doubt and fear.

I'd always stayed beside my dad
Because I feared of something bad.
I dared not step away.
So rarely did I stray.

When grazing on the mountainside,
I'd worry that I'd slip and slide,
And fall beneath the ice and snow
Into a land no one knows.

If bees and insects buzzed around,
Or inched across the stony ground,
I'd scream, "They're going to sting.
I'm scared of creepy-crawly things."

I often claimed that I was ill,
In need of medicine and a pill.
"I have got a bug. I'm feeling sick.
"I need a doctor. Please come quick!"

When asked to carry heavy packs
That farmers load on llama's backs,
I'd say, "I'm not that tough.
I'm sure I won't be strong enough."

Sometimes, I would get very mad.
My screaming would get pretty bad.

It didn't take much to make me upset.
And I'd stay steaming until the sun set.

My brothers teased me quite a lot
and often put me on the spot.
I would often get tongue-tied
And become weak and terrified.

But still, my pounding heart would quake.
My sturdy legs would start to shake.

I'd cry myself to sleep at night.
Now, something clearly wasn't right.

One day my friend, Alex, would say,
"It saddens me that you feel this way.
I'm here to help. Just come with me.
We'll conquer your anger and anxiety."

We left the mountain snow
For fields where dandelions grow.
Alex said, "Just pick a few.
And then I'll tell you what to do."

I did as Alex asked
And picked the flowers from the grass.
And then my friend said, "Hold them, so.
Now, take a breath and slowly blow."

I gently blew the seeds
Which made me very calm indeed.
As I watched them float into the air,
I didn't have a single care.

"I feel much better now," I said.
"That exercise has cleared my head.
I don't feel stressed. I don't feel weird.
My fear and anger have disappeared."

Alex was feeling very pleased.
"Yes, breathing puts your mind at ease.
To blow a dandelion, you'll find,
Will help to cure a worried mind.

Another way to keep you calm,
and this will work like a charm,
Try squeezing on a squishy toy.
I'm sure that's something you'll enjoy."

He gave me a rubber Llama
and asked me to see if it made me calmer.
"Just squeeze it hard and then release,
and soon, you'll be at perfect peace."

I squeezed and gave it a try.
Then to my worries, I said goodbye.
I felt the tension start to fade.
No longer did I feel afraid.

"Now, last of all," Alex declared,
"This trick will help you when you're scared.
Just think about your happy place.
Your fears will melt without a trace.

I did as he said, I closed my eyes.
I thought of fields with sunny skies,
Tall mountains, lakes, and rolling hills.
And deep inside, my world grew still.

And from that day, I changed.
When I felt scared or strange,
I could help ease my anxiety.
My mind and heart could be worry-free.

Anxiety happens when you think about the future
or the past. Try to live in the present. You don't have to
figure everything out all at once. Breathe.
You're strong. You got this. -E.H.

For my ninth grade teacher, May Payne, the very first person who believed I could write and draw. Thank you for believing in me, and for providing your special care.
- E.H.

Special thanks to my family and friends for which this book could not have been possible.

If you enjoyed this book, please be kind and leave an Amazon review.

I would love to hear from you at calmaLlamabooks.com

www.ingramcontent.com/pod-product-compliance
Lightning Source LLC
Chambersburg PA
CBHW042023090426
42811CB00016B/1714